Historical Atlases of South Asia,
Central Asia, and the Middle East

A HISTORICAL ATLAS OF

IRAQ

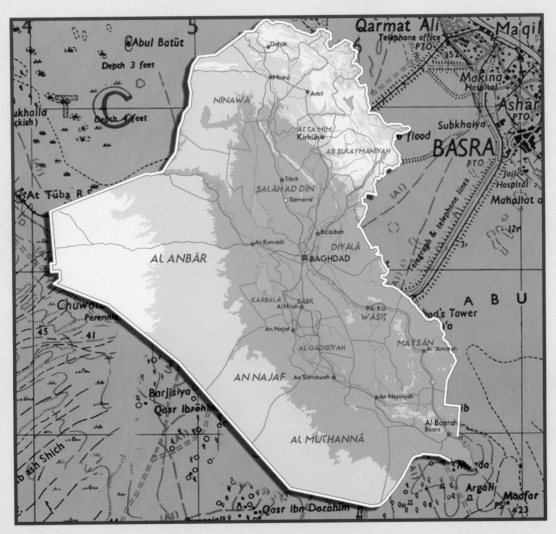

Larissa Phillips

The Rosen Publishing Group, Inc.

For Booker and Sancho

Published in 2003 by the Rosen Publishing Group, Inc.
29 East 21st Street, New York, NY 10010

Library of Congress Cataloging-in-Publication Data

Phillips, Larissa.
A Historical Atlas of Iraq / Larissa Phillips. — 1st ed.
p. cm. — (Historical Atlases of South Asia, Central Asia, and the Middle East)
Summary: Maps and text chronicle the history of the Middle Eastern nation located in a region believed to be the birthplace of civilization.
Includes bibliographical references and index.
ISBN 0-8239-3865-4
1. Iraq — History — Maps for children. 2. Iraq — Maps for children. [1. Iraq — History.
2. Atlases.] I. Title. II. Series.
G2251.S1 P4 2002
911'.567 — dc21

2002031033 2002031716

Manufactured in the United States of America

Cover image: The region that contains present-day Iraq and its city of Basra (current and twentieth-century maps, center) has been ruled by a variety of leaders since the dawn of civilization, including Mesopotamian King Hammurabi (believed to be depicted in the sculpture at bottom left), Savfavid-era shah 'Abbas I *(top left)*, and current president Saddam Hussein *(right)*.

Contents

NĪNAWĀ

Dahūk

Al Mawṣil
Mosul

Arbīl

Kirkūk

As Sulaymānīyah

Ṭikrīt

Buhayrat
ath Tharthār

Euphrates

Ba'qūbah

Ar Ramādī

AL ANBĀR

BAGHDĀD

Buhayrat
ar Razāzah

Karbalā'

KARBALĀ'

Al Ḥillah

Nahr Diālā

Al Kūt

An Najaf

AN NAJAF   As Samāwah

Euphrates

An Nāṣirīyah

SAUDI
ARABIA

Nahr Diālá

Tigris

Euphrates

INTRODUCTION

The region where present-day Iraq is located is believed to be the birthplace of civilization. Many empires have fought on its soil and claimed its territory as their own. Few, if any, regions have experienced more war, more violent political upheaval, and more ruthless campaigns to oust potential enemies. In fact, Sumerians, Assyrians, Persians, Greeks, Romans, Arabs, and Mongols have all, at one time or another, lived and prospered in the area that is now Iraq.

Today, the modern nation of Iraq wields much of its power in the global economy because of its oil reserves. Thousands of years ago, however, Iraq's land boasted a natural commodity of equal value. At that time, the region was lush with a rich, fertile soil. Such a valuable natural resource attracted scores of nomadic people, as well as armies, to its

An independent nation since 1932, Iraq was once a part of the Ottoman Empire. From 1980 to 1988, Iraq was at war with Iran over various border disputes. By 1990, Iraq had seized Kuwait, but was expelled one year later by U.S.-led forces in a conflict later known as the Persian Gulf War. Since that time, although Iraq was required to follow strict United Nations Security Council (UNSC) controls, including a continuous examination of Iraqi weapons, the country has failed to respond to weapons inspectors. In September 2002, according to Reuters, advisors to Iraqi president Saddam Hussein claimed that UN weapons inspectors will have "unfettered access to any site they want to inspect in Iraq."

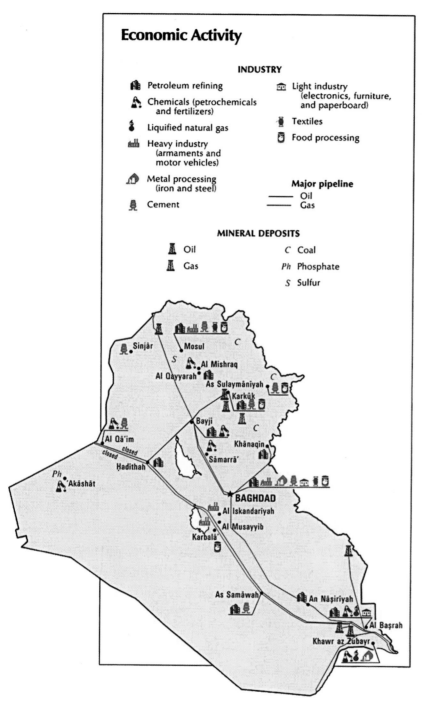

Economic Activity

INDUSTRY

- Petroleum refining
- Chemicals (petrochemicals and fertilizers)
- Liquified natural gas
- Heavy industry (armaments and motor vehicles)
- Metal processing (iron and steel)
- Cement

- Light industry (electronics, furniture, and paperboard)
- Textiles
- Food processing

Major pipeline
—— Oil
—— Gas

MINERAL DEPOSITS

- Oil
- Gas

- C   Coal
- Ph Phosphate
- S   Sulfur

Sinjâr   Mosul   C
S
Al Mishraq
Al Qayyarah
As Sulaymânîyah
Karkûk   C
Bayji   C
Al Qâ'im
closed   Khânaqîn
closed   Sâmarrâ'
Hadîthah
Ph
'Akâshât
BAGHDAD
Al Iskandarîyah
Al Musayyib
Karbalâ'
As Samâwah   An Nâsirîyah
Al Basrah
Khawr az Zubayr

Iraq's economy is driven by its oil exports, as illustrated in this 1993 U.S. map by the Central Intelligence Agency (CIA). Still reeling from economic setbacks brought on by the Iran-Iraq War that totaled an estimated $100 billion, Iraq has since benefited from the UN oil-for-food program that allowed the country to exchange limited amounts of oil with foreign nations for much-needed food and medicine. By 1999, the UN Security Council expanded the flagship program, a decision that raised the overall standard of living in Iraq.

lands. These people prospered and eventually created wondrous cities and empires in the Middle East.

Archaeologists discovered the ruins of ancient Sumer just 150 years ago, allowing scholars to gain a new understanding of ancient civilizations. Part of Mesopotamia, an ancient civilization that once thrived on Iraq's lands, it is considered the cradle of human civilization.

Because the political climate in the Middle East is presently unstable, and given the rise of fundamentalist Islamic terrorism around the world, many countries such as the United States are now focusing their attention on the Arab nations. With the United States's dependency on the Middle East for its oil, and the threat of Saddam Hussein's potential weapons of mass destruction, knowledge of Iraq's history is essential.

1 THE SUMERIAN CIVILIZATION

Historians speculate that nowhere in the world has geography played such a dramatic role in the shaping of a region's history than in what is now Iraq. Greek historians named it Mesopotamia, meaning "the [land] between the rivers." The Tigris and Euphrates Rivers, both of which flow into southern Iraq, played a dramatic role in Mesopotamian history. Perhaps if the area had been a mountainous region like the Himalayas, or an island like Great Britain, the victors in each war might have retained power. But the Mesopotamian Plain is flat and unprotected. There are no mountains or jungles to protect defending armies, nor oceans to exhaust and defeat invading armies.

In times of peace, the Tigris and Euphrates Rivers brought both success and devastation to the people of Mesopotamia. On the one hand, rich soil deposits created fertile farmland, causing people to migrate to Mesopotamian lands from all directions. On the other hand, proximity to volatile rivers meant that unpredictable, terrible flooding periodically destroyed those same rich, fertile cities.

The Sumerian civilization began to blossom in southern Iraq between 3500 and 3000 BC. Primitive dwellings were built from bricks made of clay, which was plentiful. The Sumerians also built temples for

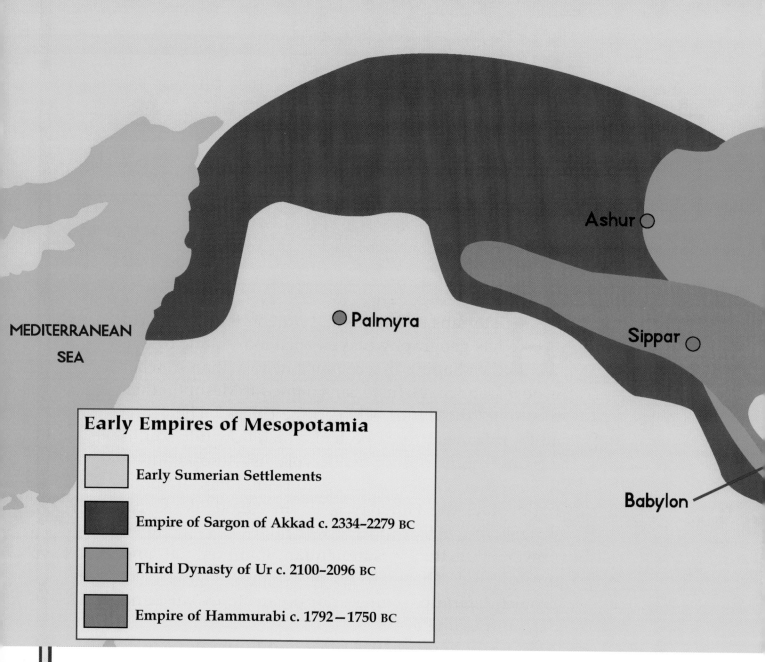

Ashur ○

○ Palmyra

Sippar ○

MEDITERRANEAN
SEA

Early Empires of Mesopotamia

Early Sumerian Settlements

Empire of Sargon of Akkad c. 2334–2279 BC

Third Dynasty of Ur c. 2100–2096 BC

Empire of Hammurabi c. 1792—1750 BC

Babylon

The lands of Mesopotamia are aptly referred to as the Fertile Crescent because of the region's ability to sustain agriculture. Beyond basic needs such as water, food, and shelter, Sumerians, who once occupied southern Iraq, had an organized workforce that grew a variety of crops and herded sheep and cattle for food, meat, and milk. This modern model of an ancient ziggurat *(upper right)* was typical of Sumerian temples for worshiping.

worshiping, called ziggurats, which were similar to early step pyramids.

Early Achievements

One of the greatest feats of the Sumerians was the development of the first known written language, later called cuneiform. Using a full alphabet, the Sumerians inscribed letters on wet clay with a sharp reed used as a stylus, and then baked the tablet in the sun. Because writing curved lines on

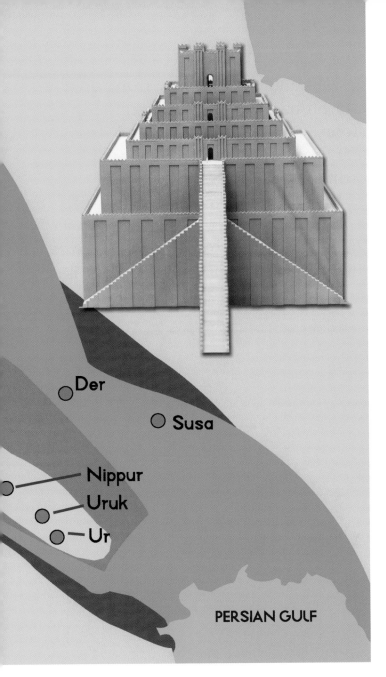

Der

Susa

Nippur

Uruk

Ur

PERSIAN GULF

fact, the Sumerians developed the double entry accounting method that is still used today.

The invention of the wheel, also credited to the Sumerians, caused dramatic gains in productivity as much as any other of their achievements had. They developed plows made of bronze and used oxen to pull them. For the first time, food such as wheat was farmed more easily and then transported. The Sumerians traded stores of food and other goods; their culture prospered.

With a surplus of both food and goods, the Sumerians had time to explore ideas like mathematics. Their system was based on the number sixty. The sixty-minute hour and the concept of 360 degrees in a circle originated with the Sumerians. A relatively peaceful people, they also created a judicial system. Mutilation and execution were not uncommon, but every Sumerian citizen had access to legal counsel and due process before a judge.

Other accomplishments of the Sumerians include the calendar, astronomical theories, and a mix of surgery and magic that they called medicine. Since surgeons were held literally accountable for a patient's outcome (if the patient lost an eye in surgery, for example, the surgeon's eye would be removed, too), it is not

small clay tablets was so difficult, the cuneiform letters were wedge-shaped.

Developing a written language and early methods of counting meant that the Sumerians could record transactions. They passed information to future generations, which furthered their cultural and agricultural gains. They developed accounting practices, which increased trading. In

surprising that Sumerian surgeons relied heavily on spells, trying to avoid surgery at all costs.

The Sumerians also employed forms of architecture such as the dome, the arch, the vault, and the column, all of which would not be used in the Western world for thousands of years. Sumerian artisans crafted vessels and adornments from gold and bronze to lapis lazuli and soapstone, which they imported from afar. Copper was commonly used for ordinary objects.

Even with all their progress, life in Sumer was hard and unpredictable, a fact reflected in Sumerian literature. The *Epic of Gilgamesh* is

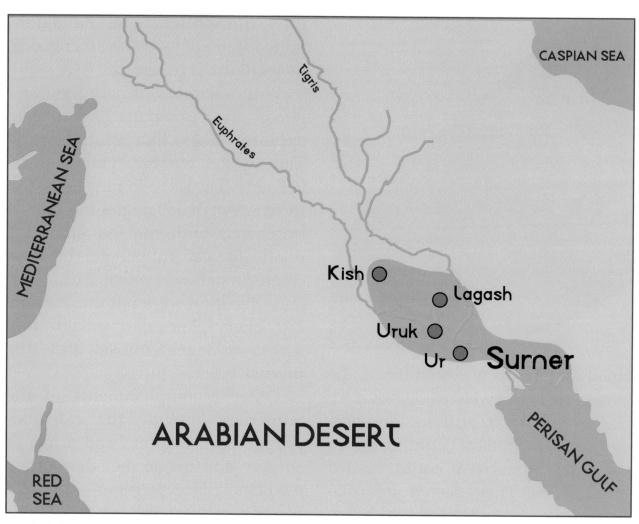

Although the Sumerians frequently battled the flooding waters of the Tigris and Euphrates Rivers, they eventually harnessed the rivers' power with a series of canals and levees that helped to irrigate their plentiful crops. Uruk, seen on this map, was the largest of the Sumerian city-states and had an estimated population of 10,000. Like other city-states, Uruk had a main temple (ziggurat) that was surrounded by various courts and public buildings. Less important private structures, all of which were made from mud brick, were built out from the center of the city.

The ancient seals and tablets pictured here are written in cuneiform, a simple form of pictographic writing developed by the Sumerians. These clay tablets depict animals slain in a hunt, worshipers led before gods, and various scenes of daily life. The center tablet is an early multiplication table. The word "cuneiform" means "wedge-shaped" because of the shape of the instruments that were used to write the language onto wet slabs of clay. Young boys of wealthy parents usually learned cuneiform in a school called an *edubba*, or "tablet house."

the best-known Sumerian work. The story of Gilgamesh, King of Uruk, relates his wish for immortality. The *Epic*, which predates the Bible, also includes a detailed story of a devastating flood in which only one man was warned. In the story the man builds a boat, fills it with animals, and waits out the flood for seven days.

Some archeologists believe that the story of Noah, his ark, and the great flood, found in the Old Testament of the Bible, was based on one particularly terrible flood in the Mesopotamian Valley. Others argue that the flood was simply a Mesopotamian myth. Both historians and archaeologists are certain, however, that the ancient Sumerians were familiar with flooding waters. They gradually learned to protect themselves from the constant overflow of river currents by building great walls around their cities. They also built structures on elevated platforms. The Akkadians,

enemies of the Sumerians who lived to the north, were more devastated by flood waters. The destruction of these less advanced tribes and towns probably gave the Sumerians the ability to advance.

Despite the accomplished society of the Sumerians, the culture was eventually overcome. Constant warfare among the people of the various city-states within the region resulted in continuous fighting. Around 2400 BC, the Akkadians from northern Mesopotamia conquered the territory of Sumer. The most advanced civilization yet became captive to its longtime enemies.

2 THE AKKADIANS

Most historians believe that the Akkadians were Semitic nomads from central Iraq. It is thought that they migrated south over the Arabian Peninsula and periodically invaded Mesopotamia. They had a fierce reputation as warriors, and were eventually able to control all of Sumer.

The Akkadians spoke a Semitic language, which is as different from the Sumerian language as Italian is from Chinese. Today, the word "Semitic" is often thought to mean Jewish. However, it originally referred to people who spoke any of a group of related languages, such as Hebrew and Arabic, which are still used today, or Assyrian and Babylonian, which are now ancient. The Akkadians completely adapted the Sumerian cuneiform to their own language.

MEDITERRANEAN SEA

RED SEA

The Akkadian civilization, as seen on this map, was one that conquered and absorbed Sumerian city-states before expanding the empire in a northwest direction from present-day Saudi Arabia to present-day Lebanon. The Akkadians remained powerful until 2125 BC when the Sumerian city of Ur rose in revolt. That, along with growing power from neighboring Guti tribes, finally disabled the Akkadians around 2000 BC, giving way to what would later be called the Neo-Sumerian Period.

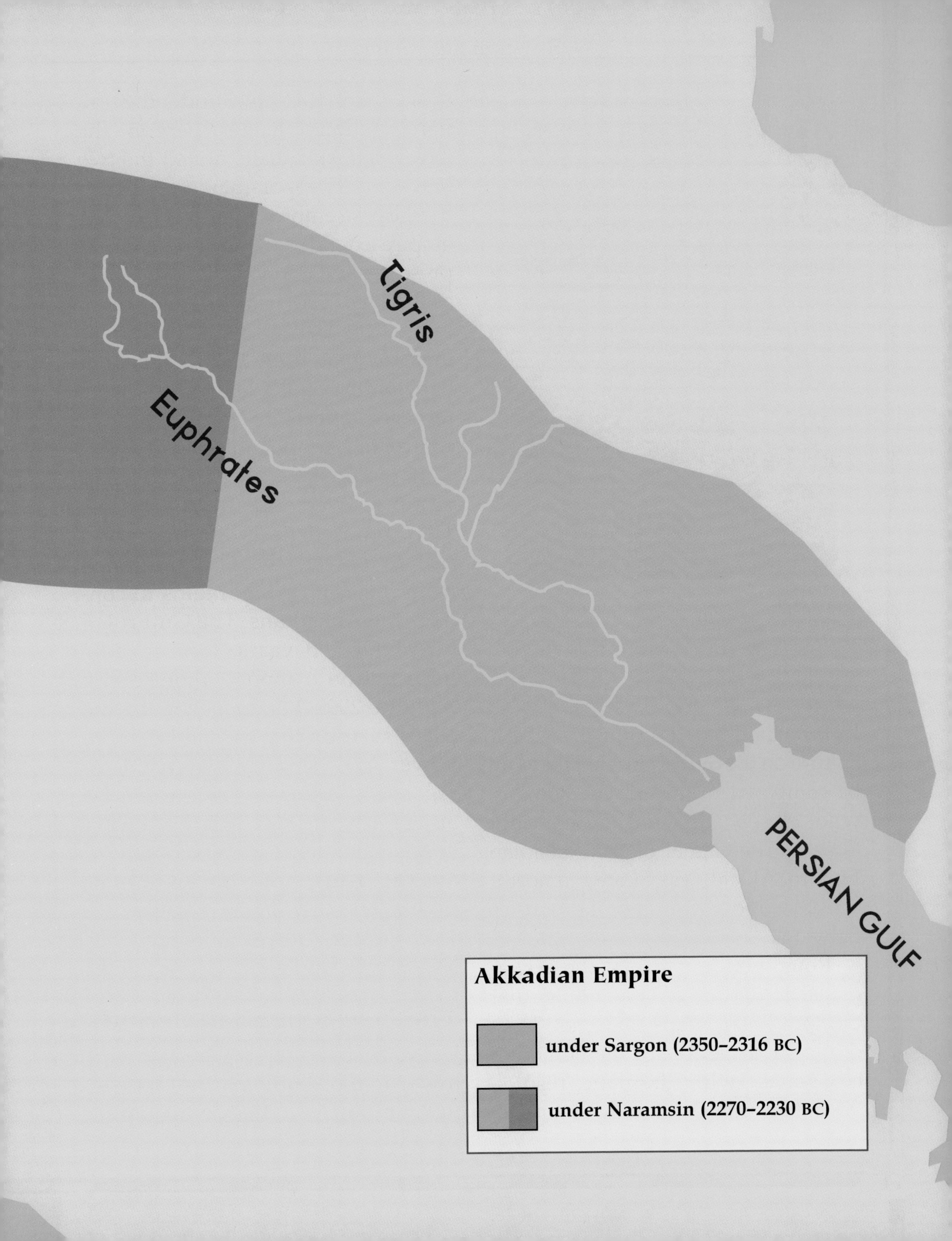

Tigris

Euphrates

PERSIAN GULF

Akkadian Empire

under Sargon (2350–2316 BC)

under Naramsin (2270–2230 BC)

This clay tablet is one example of Akkadian cuneiform writing. It is actually a letter from an Egyptian leader to a Palestinian chief and dates from the eighteenth Egyptian dynasty, approximately 1515 BC, or the start of the New Kingdom in Egypt.

In fact, they based so much of their culture on the Sumerians that they can be compared to the ancient Romans, who closely imitated the ancient Greeks. The capital of the Akkadian Empire, Akkad, was located in northern Mesopotamia, later known as Babylon.

Roughhewn warriors, the Akkadians accomplished one thing that the gentle Sumerians could not: They diminished the role of the Sumerian city-states, with dramatic results. Akkadian rule lasted only about 200 years, but in that time, under the brilliant military leader Sargon the Great, the Akkadians united the two halves of Mesopotamia, establishing the largest empire then known. The empire extended to the north as far as present-day Turkey, to the west as far as the Mediterranean Sea, and southeast to the Persian Gulf. Historians theorize that until the final fall of Babylon in 539 BC, all conflicts were renewed efforts to recapture total control of Mesopotamia.

It would take an even stronger group to overcome the Akkadians. Two hundred years after Sargon's rise to power, the Guti migrated from the Zagros Mountains to conquer the Akkadians. The Guti ruled for about 100 years, leaving little information about themselves. Around 2000 BC, however, in the chaos surrounding the Gutis' rise to power, the Sumerians were able to regain power. The people of the Sumerian city of Ur, located in what is now the southern region of Iraq on the banks of the Euphrates River, revolted against the Guti. This conflict paved the way the Neo-Sumerian Period.

The Neo-Sumerian Period

Ur-Nammu, leader of the Sumerians toward the end of the second millennium, was highly successful in restoring the Sumerian Empire. In the short time that he ruled, Ur-Nammu established what is believed to be the earliest collection of laws. He built new temples, including an enormous ziggurat. After his death, Ur-Nammu's son, and then grandson, took power, controlling a larger empire. The Sumerians established administrative units for governing and collecting taxes, and separated military and political power. Communication and trade flourished as traders traveled roads that were protected by fortresses.

Inevitably, this period of Sumerian growth lasted only about 120 years. A tribal people from the desert regions of Arabia and Syria, called the Amorites, began attacking the western frontier, making their way into the Sumerian Empire. For the next 200 years, the territory once ruled by the Sumerians was divided into four sections. It took Hammurabi, the next great leader, to unite the region once again.

The Babylonian Empire

King Hammurabi, who reigned from 1792 to 1750 BC, united the four

Sargon the Great

While the Sumerians believed their rulers were servants of the gods, the Akkadians thought of their rulers as gods themselves. Naturally, a cult of mythology began to surround Sargon the Great (2371–2316 BC), with myths and legends to explain his origins. According to tradition, Sargon had been born in secrecy, placed in a reed basket, and floated down the Euphrates River where a farmer found him and raised him as his son. This legend has also been ascribed to Krishna, Moses, and other great men who may have come from humble backgrounds. Later, after conquering all of Sumer, legend has it that Sargon washed his weapons in the Persian Gulf, an indication that he had conquered the southern region of the Middle East.

The Akkadian sculpture seen here is one of only two surviving works from the period, both currently housed in the Iraq Museum in Baghdad. Some scholars believe it depicts Sargon the Great.

kingdoms of Mesopotamia, establishing the city of Babylon as the new capital. Called the King of the Four Quarters of the World, Hammurabi ruled during a period known as the First Dynasty of Babylon.

Hammurabi's main concerns were protecting the Mesopotamian borders and establishing peace, prosperity, and justice throughout his kingdom. By interpreting the tablets that still exist today, historians believe that Hammurabi was a skilled and diplomatic leader, peacefully uniting the Assyrians and the Babylonians.

Although Hammurabi respected past myths and traditions, he did so in a progressive manner. He restored temples and adapted myths to his own liking, making himself the center of power. Finally, he ordered that the formerly modest palace be rebuilt into an enormous complex of reception rooms, living spaces, and secured storage areas.

Hammurabi believed in harsh punishments such as death, bodily mutilation, and beating, but he also believed that the state should protect the weak from the powerful. He expected that social justice would be available to every man. After Hammurabi's death in 1750 BC, however, the Babylonian Empire declined.

A century and a half after Hammurabi's death, the Hittites conquered Babylon, then quickly departed. Another group, the Kassites, with an army of horsemen, established control over the empire. The Kassites ruled for 400 years and divided the land into two territories: Babylon in the north, and Assyria in the south. In this way, Babylon ceased to be politically centralized, although it remained a cultural capital for the entire region.

Despite the decline of Babylon, the Kassite rule represented a period of

Hammurabi, believed to be depicted in this sculpture from the Babylonian period, is remembered for his ancient Law Code, improved irrigation systems, the restoration of existing cities and their temples, and a regulation of tribute payments and the food supply.

The Code of Hammurabi

Hammurabi's greatest legacy is his code of ancient laws. The code, which dealt with about 282 decisions handed down by the king during his reign, still exists. Its most basic element is expressed in the phrase "an eye for an eye; a tooth for a tooth." Near the end of his reign, Hammurabi ordered that his laws and decisions be set in stone and placed inside temples. One such copy was inscribed on a giant slab of black diorite. Archaeologists unearthed the ancient slab in Susa, Iraq (formerly the ancient city of Elam), in the early 1900s.

The great Mesopotamian king Hammurabi was respected as an accomplished leader. The top of this slab found in Susa (*right*) features Hammurabi dictating his laws to a scribe. The actual laws are inscribed below the relief.

revival for the whole of Mesopotamia. Temples were built and others that had fallen into ruin were restored. Order, stability, and peace were brought back to a land that had been at war for centuries. The Kassites were skilled riders. They introduced the horse as an animal for both fighting and transportation, revolutionizing many aspects of ancient life. Kassite traders commonly traveled on horseback to surrounding cities to trade goods. Mesopotamian goods such as sesame oil, textiles, and resin were traded in local and distant cities for gold, lapis lazuli, and ivory.

While the Kassites remained peaceful, wars and border disputes were raging beyond the edge of their territory. By 1160 BC, a people called the Elamites invaded Mesopotamia and brought the Kassite empire to its knees. The vast Elamite army swiftly traveled across southern Mesopotamia and sacked Babylon in the north.

Monuments of great cultural significance—such as the Code of Hammurabi and a statue of the god Marduk—were taken to the Elamites' home city of Susa. This great, symbolic insult was replayed again and again over time.

3 THE ASSYRIAN EMPIRE

MEDITERRANEAN SEA

RED SEA

Victory was short-lived for the Elamites. In the south, during the ninth century BC, a new Babylonian dynasty was founded. Its king, Nebuchadnezzar I, attacked the city of Elam and took its treasures, including the stolen statue of Marduk. Yet victory in Mesopotamia was brief. Assyrian armies invaded Elam and also advanced from the north, preparing to battle for Mesopotamian territory.

Under King Tiglath-Pileser I (1115–1077 BC), Assyria controlled its enemies, conquering them and extending its border to Syria, and on to the Mediterranean Sea. But when total domination seemed assured, the murder of Tiglath-Pileser brought several centuries of chaos, war, and famine to the region.

By 1000 BC, Assyria was in its darkest era. It had lost access to valuable trading routes. Total defeat was spared only because the Aramaeans were too busy fighting each other to

Despite its sleepy beginnings as an empire, the Assyrian conquest of southern Mesopotamia would eventually spread west through present-day Syria, sections of Saudi Arabia, and finally Palestine. The Assyrian Empire was unique in that it continually forced the people it conquered to the outer edges of its territories. This forced migration of foreign people into new territory enhanced Assyrian culture, turning the entire region into one that was a mix of various languages and social customs.

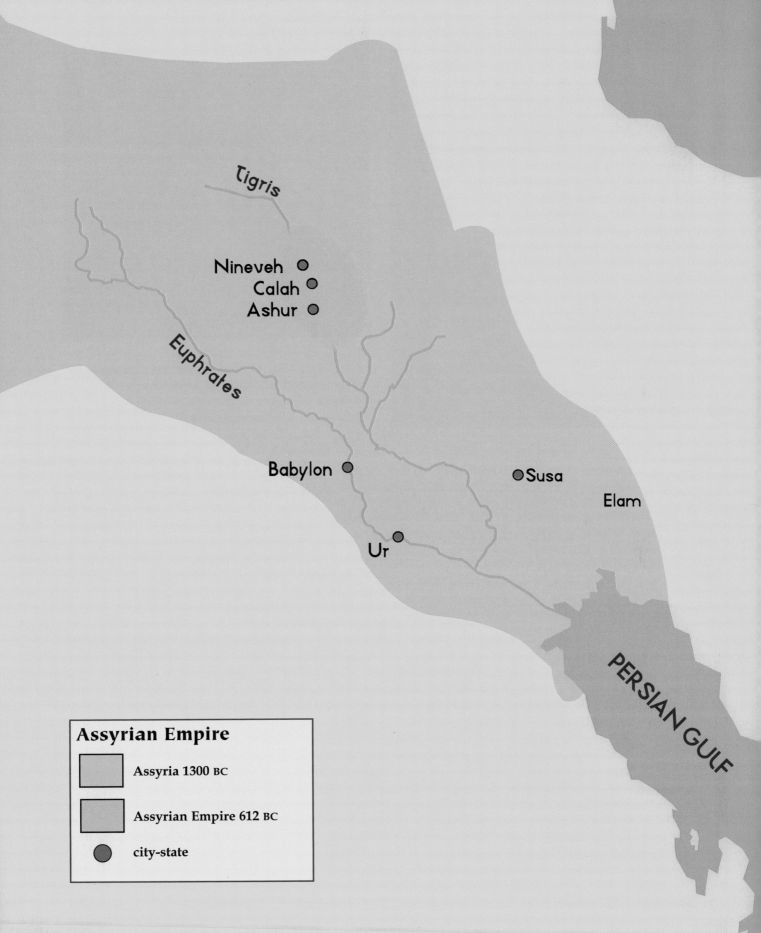

Tigris

Nineveh ○

Calah ○

Ashur ○

Euphrates

Babylon ●

Susa ●

Elam

Ur ●

PERSIAN GULF

Assyrian Empire

Assyria 1300 BC

Assyrian Empire 612 BC

● city-state

The sculptures pictured here are taken from the Palace of Sargon II (reigned 721–705 BC), the Assyrian king thought by scholars to be the younger son of Tiglath-Pileser III. Like other Assyrian kings before him, Sargon II was responsible for expanding the empire.

conquer Assyria. Economically suffering, Assyria had lost territory. The Aramaeans had tents pitched near the gates of the city of Assur.

Despite Assyria's losses, its long history of war had taught its soldiers well. Its dynasty—unbroken for some 200 years—had great advantages. The Assyrians had horses and weapons, and they were born warriors.

Finally, in the midst of chaos, Assyria awakened to its full potential. Seeking both the income and the safety that defeating their enemies brought them, the Assyrians also sought a religious victory.

The Assyrians fought mercilessly across the land. In 911 BC, they expelled the Aramaeans from the valley. Assyrian armies, along with King Ashurnasirpal II, reclaimed cities, including Babylon. Resistors were tortured, massacred, and enslaved. By 884 BC, Assyria occupied the northern section of present-day Iraq. With its newfound victories, Assyria began the conversion from kingdom to empire.

Assyrian Dominance

Ashurnasirpal II became known for both his ambition and his cruelty. Archaeologists have found various narratives engraved throughout Ashurnasirpal's massive palace that likely inspired obedience in his fearful subjects. In an era known for its brutality, men, women, and children in Ashurnasirpal's day were subjected to sadistic forms of torture, such as flaying, dismemberment, and impaling. Warriors were burned alive. Many others were imprisoned in the desert to die of dehydration. Perhaps just as cruel, Ashurnasirpal methodically recorded torture to demonstrate his dominance.

Shalmaneser III, Ashurnasirpal's warlike son and successor, ruled the empire for approximately thirty-five years, most of which were spent fighting. Under Shalmaneser, the Assyrians gained land, traveling ever farther in search of territories to raid. Soon their targets were other powerful kingdoms in present-day Iran and Egypt. Once victorious, the Assyrians established their own government in these kingdoms to suppress uprisings and collect taxes. In this way, Assyria became a wealthy empire. But Assyrian leaders cared

This relief sculpture was originally a part of the ancient Assyrian palace of Ashurnasirpal II, the ruler of Assyria from 884–859 BC. Much of what historians know about Ashurnasirpal was learned from his own inscriptions, many of which were found among the ruins of his palace in the ancient city of Calah (present-day Nirud, Iraq). During his reign he had the city completely rebuilt with many temples, shrines, and lavish botanical gardens.

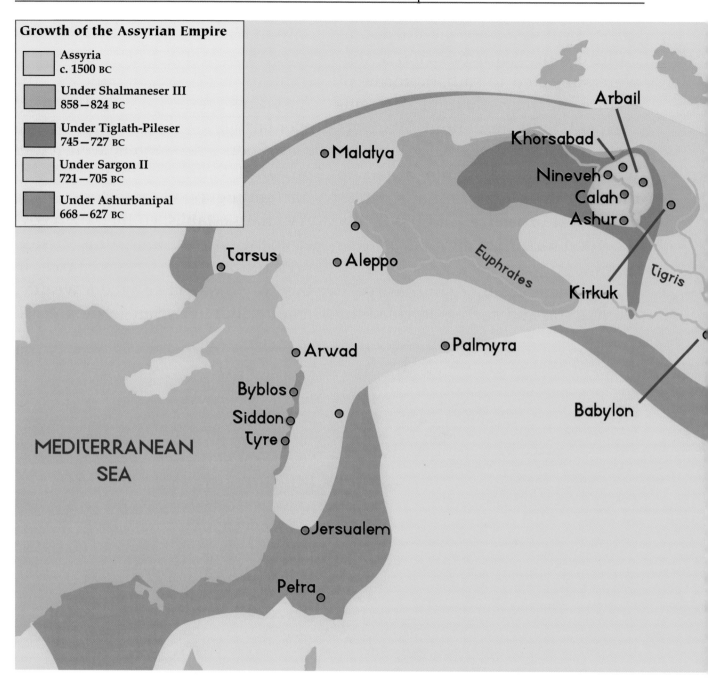

Growth of the Assyrian Empire

Assyria
c. 1500 BC

Under Shalmaneser III
858 — 824 BC

Under Tiglath-Pileser
745 — 727 BC

Under Sargon II
721 — 705 BC

Under Ashurbanipal
668 — 627 BC

Malatya

Arbail

Khorsabad

Nineveh

Calah

Ashur

Tarsus

Aleppo

Euphrates

Tigris

Kirkuk

Arwad

Palmyra

Byblos

Siddon

Tyre

Babylon

MEDITERRANEAN
SEA

Jersualem

Petra

Though many Assyrian kings expanded the empire's territory, as illustrated on this map, a few are remembered for actions other than conquest. Sargon II, for instance, continued the Assyrian practice of dispersing conquered peoples from their settlements by forcing the Hebrews from Israel. His decision marks the beginning of the Jewish Diaspora, or the breaking up and scattering of people from their ancestral homelands. Ashurbanipal, on the other hand, is best remembered for assembling one of the greatest libraries of the ancient world, of which 30,000 stone tablets remain. His accomplishment stands as the single greatest source of recorded Mesopotamian history.

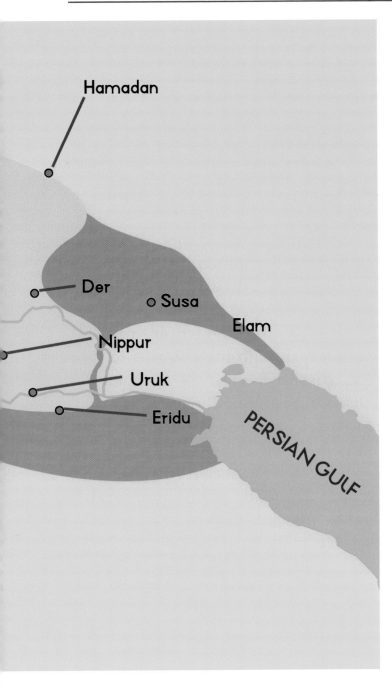

the king, taking twenty-seven cities. Shalmaneser assisted another son, Shamshi-Adad V, in stopping the uprising. Civil war raged within Assyria for four years, ending with Shalmaneser's death. The king's son Shamshi-Adad V took the throne.

Shamshi-Adad died an early death, leaving his young son Adad-nirari III as king. But because the prince was still young, his mother, Sammuramat, took his place. The Greek historian Herodotus described Sammuramat as "the most beautiful, most cruel, most powerful, and most lustful of Oriental queens." When Adad-nirari III, and later his sons, finally took the throne, the Assyrian Empire began to decline.

More than fifty years later, King Tiglath-Pileser III helped Assyria regain its glory and power. A meticulous master of organization, he rebuilt the Assyrian army, defeated Assyria's enemies at the border, and established ultimate power over Assyria's more distant territories. Tiglath-Pileser did this by transforming newly acquired lands into provinces, placing their leaders under the supervision of an Assyrian administrator. He called for mass deportations of people, which broke their spirit and crushed any chance of uprising. In 744 BC, in one campaign alone, some 65,000 people were expelled from a Persian province

little for their subjects. Impoverished and poorly treated, people constantly threatened to rebel. Their discontent ultimately undermined the empire.

Near the end of Shalmaneser's reign in 824 BC, his eldest son, Ashur-danin-apla, revolted against while 150,000 people were pushed out of southern Mesopotamia. Ultimately this forced exodus backfired, causing such misery among the displaced people that anti-Assyrian sentiment increased.

In 721 BC, Sargon II assumed the throne. He further strengthened the empire, moved the capital to Dur-Sharrukin (present-day Khorsabad), and built an exquisite palace-temple. It towered over the city on a platform fifty feet (fifteen meters) high. Blue-glazed bricks lined the palace; ornate frescoes depicted stories on walls that stretched 1.5 miles (2.5 kilometers)

This sculptured relief, taken from the Palace of Ashurbanipal in Ninevah, depicts Assyrian armies scaling the walls in a campaign against the ancient city of Elam. It is now housed in the Louvre Museum in Paris, France.

long. There was a seven-story ziggu-rat—each level a different color—encircled with a spiral ramp. But the splendor was abandoned almost immediately when Sargon was killed during battle. Sargon's son and heir, Sennacherib, abandoned the palace complex, and relocated the capital to Nineveh.

Sargon's descendants, a people called the Sargonids, ruled Assyria for the next 100 years, beginning in 668 with king Ashurbanipal. Under their leadership the empire reached its peak, though it continued to face the dissatisfaction of its people. Discontent among the people turned to hatred, and the empire grew too large to be effectively governed.

Still, the Assyrian Empire had made dramatic and measurable gains. Its influence, especially in science, mathematics, and astronomy, was felt as far away as the Macedonian Empire in present-day Greece. Assyrians had also engineered a system of canals and aqueducts. Culturally, they excelled at sculpture, painting, and even political propaganda. But like all empires, Assyria was poised to fall, and finally did so in 612 BC.

4 THE FALL OF MESOPOTAMIA

While the Assyrians had been overextending their boundaries, two allies—the Medes and the Chaldeans—had taken over Babylonia around 609 BC. When the Medes and the Chaldeans combined their forces and turned their attention to Assyria, it took them just three years to devastate an empire that had ruled for three centuries.

The Medes fought ruthlessly, gaining wealth and leaving to conquer new lands. The Chaldeans, in contrast, revitalized Babylon and remained there. Soon it was the largest and most beautiful city in the East. At that point, Egypt largely controlled Syria and Palestine, preventing the Chaldeans from gaining access to the West for trading. But an ambitious young crown prince, Nebuchadnezzar II (also known as Nebuchadrezzar II), took on the task of defeating the Egyptians. In 597 BC, by then the king of Babylonia, Nebuchadnezzar defeated the Egyptians and captured Jerusalem, deporting and enslaving thousands of Jews to Mesopotamia.

At the time, Babylon was a glorious capital city. Long considered a sacred area, it is not surprising that Babylon had undergone a renaissance that had taken the form of a religious revival. Sacred temples were a major center of social and economic influence. The Chaldeans revived spirituality, enacting age-old

The Hanging Gardens of Babylon, one of the Seven Wonders of the Ancient World, are depicted in this sixteenth-century drawing by Maarten van Heemskerck, a work that is currently housed in the Louvre Museum in Paris, France.

ceremonies. Architecturally, Babylon was splendid. A giant protective wall surrounded the city. The wall was such that four horses could draw chariots each adjacent to the others along the top. The fortress wall was beautifully decorated with intricate designs of enameled bricks. Eight huge thoroughfares from inside the city's walls led to the outside world through ornate portals, including the Ishtar Gate, which was decorated with fiery red dragons.

Perhaps the most amazing structure in the ancient city was the Hanging Gardens of Babylon, considered one of the Seven Wonders of the Ancient World. The gardens were a lavish tribute built by Nebuchadnezzar II for his wife,

Amytis, the Medean princess who missed her homeland. The gardens consisted of lush tropical foliage climbing to the roof of the palace, which seemed to be hanging layers of terraces. Water from the Euphrates River was pumped into the garden through a complex mechanical irrigation system.

The luxurious living conditions of the people of Babylon, however, threatened to put the city in debt. In response, Nebuchadnezzar imposed heavy taxes on his subjects. He created a standardized system of currency, which allowed for the development of credit. In essence, capitalism was born in Babylon. Private business became possible, and some families became wealthy.

But as splendid and progressive as Babylon was, it was not well defended. In 539 BC, Cyrus, king of the Persians, captured the city. Although the Persians occupied its boundaries and tried to keep it

This sixteenth-century oil painting, *The Tower of Babel* by Flemish artist Pieter Brueghel the Elder, is a medieval example of a fantastic ziggurat. The story of the Tower of Babel, and mankind's attempt to ascend to the heavens, is closely related to the goals of Mesopotamian builders of the same design. Brueghel based his design of the tower on the Roman Colosseum, which he had visited. This painting is now housed in the Kunsthistorisches Museum in Vienna, Austria.

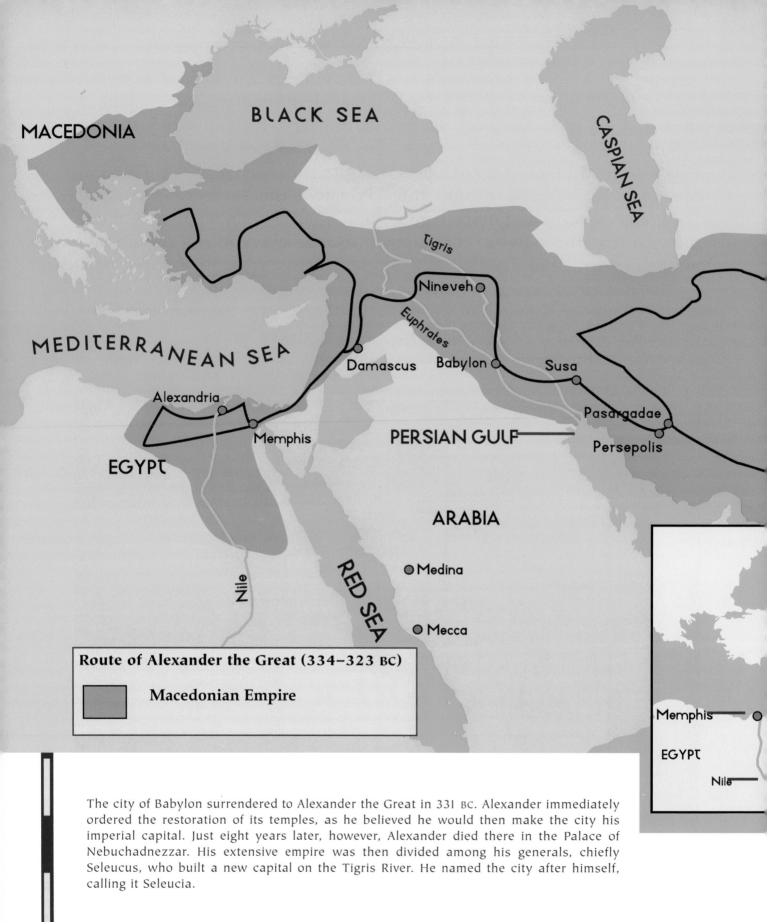

MACEDONIA

BLACK SEA

CASPIAN SEA

Tigris

Nineveh

MEDITERRANEAN SEA

Euphrates

Damascus

Babylon

Susa

Alexandria

PERSIAN GULF

Pasargadae

Memphis

Persepolis

EGYPT

ARABIA

Nile

Medina

RED SEA

Mecca

Route of Alexander the Great (334–323 BC)

Macedonian Empire

Memphis

EGYPT

Nile

The city of Babylon surrendered to Alexander the Great in 331 BC. Alexander immediately ordered the restoration of its temples, as he believed he would then make the city his imperial capital. Just eight years later, however, Alexander died there in the Palace of Nebuchadnezzar. His extensive empire was then divided among his generals, chiefly Seleucus, who built a new capital on the Tigris River. He named the city after himself, calling it Seleucia.

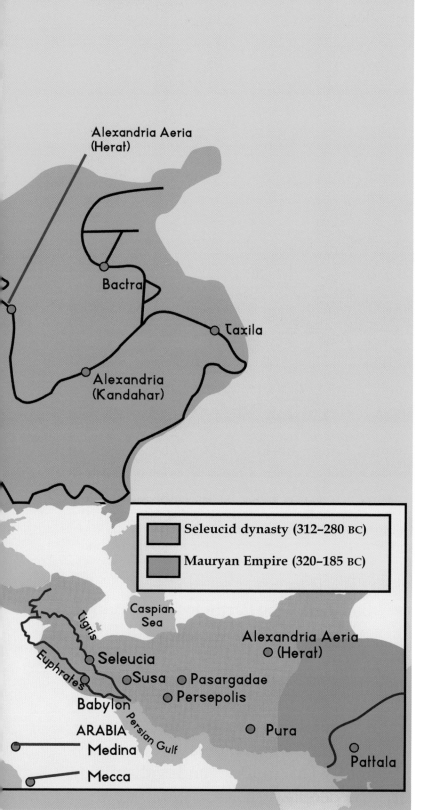

Alexandria Aeria
(Herat)

Bactra

Taxila

Alexandria
(Kandahar)

Seleucid dynasty (312–280 BC)

Mauryan Empire (320–185 BC)

Caspian
Sea

Tigris

Euphrates

Alexandria Aeria
O (Herat)

Seleucia

Susa O Pasargadae
O Persepolis

Babylon

ARABIA

Persian Gulf

Medina

Pura

Pattala

Mecca

running, the city fell into gradual decline. By 600 AD, more than a thousand years after the Persian occupation began, the city had been abandoned and lay in ruins.

The Death of a Civilization

The years following the invasion of Babylon by Cyrus the Great of Persia are known as the Achaemenid Period. After Cyrus's death, his successors focused on fighting the Egyptians, and later the Macedonians, or Greeks. The Persians, now the rulers of the Mesopotamian region, called for Aramaic to be the language of the land. Soon the common people of Babylonia forgot their own language, and with it their history. Scholars and scribes were the only subjects who could still read Akkadian and Sumerian cuneiform script.

The Hellenistic Period began during the fourth century BC with the arrival of Alexander the Great, the Macedonian soldier who set out to conquer the world. The Persian armies surrendered easily. Alexander was welcomed by the people of the city as a liberator from the hated Persians, and was immediately crowned

Pictured here is the tomb of Cyrus the Great (590–529 BC), founder of the Persian Empire, located in Pasrgadae, the earliest capital of Persia. Translations of several historical accounts tell of Alexander the Great's travels in Persia (Iran) and how he found Cyrus's tomb broken into and robbed of its contents. The accounts also convey that Alexander, deeply disturbed by the desecration, ordered the tomb repaired and resealed shortly before his own death in 323 BC.

king. Although Alexander had elaborate plans for Babylon, they were cut short by his death in 323 BC at the age of thirty-three.

Alexander's successors proved less capable of holding the empire together. The Greeks founded other cities, too, and gradually Babylon lost importance as a cultural capital.

By 122 BC, the Parthians took control, followed by the Sassanians of Persia during the third century AD. Battles and warfare ensued for the next several centuries with no lasting victor. Essentially leaderless and unstable, the area was vulnerable for a new means of uniting and galvanizing the people.

5 ARAB CONQUESTS

In AD 637, the Arabs conquered the Persians, ushering a new era into the Mesopotamian region. The Arabs were originally a nomadic people who traveled from the Arabian Peninsula. They became followers of the prophet Muhammad, who preached Islam, the youngest of the world's five most widespread religions. When Muhammad died, a crisis ensued over the choice of his caliph, or successor.

One possibility was Muhammad's father-in-law, Abu Bakr, who had been the prophet's first disciple. Another possibility was Muhammad's cousin and son-in-law, Ali, who had married Muhammad's daughter, Fatimah. Abu Bakr was elected as caliph. This decision led to serious consequences, eventually causing Muslims to split into two factions, the Sunnis and the Shiites. In the meantime, under their new caliph, the Muslims traveled farther north and began raiding Mesopotamia, gathering wealth and followers.

When Abu Bakr died, he was replaced by Umar ibn al-Khattab, another Sunni. Umar preached that Islam should be viewed as a holy war, or *jihad*, against people who practice other religions. The Muslims were a small army of ragged tribesmen on horses and camels, but they were also skilled fighters. They conquered both the Byzantine and the Persian Empires, and then took the cities of Jerusalem and

ASIAE NOVA DESCRIPTIO.

This sixteenth-century map of south Asia gives the modern reader a clear idea of the typical distortion of the continent as earlier cartographers recorded it. A map such as this was possibly included in the first edition of Dutch cartographer Abraham Ortelius's *Theatrum Orbis Terrarum*, now considered the first modern atlas. Recalled today for its detail, and in cases such as this for its inaccuracy, Ortelius commonly used his maps as well as those of other cartographers. After Ortelius's death, more than forty editions of his atlas were printed from 1570 to 1624, including translations from Dutch into Latin, German, Spanish, French, Italian, and English.

Ctesiphon (or Al Madain) in AD 637. With these victories secured, they pressed east toward Afghanistan. In AD 644, while in India, Umar was murdered by a Persian slave.

Uthman succeeded Umar as caliph. Uthman founded the Umayyad dynasty, which extended from China in the east, across northern Africa, and as far north as present-day Spain. But Uthman was a weak leader; soon the people of Kufa, the first Muslim city, rose up against him. Like Umar before him, Uthman was also killed by people who believed that Ali should be caliph.

Ali, Muhammad's cousin and son-in-law, was chosen as the next caliph. He was a gentle, pious man, but he led two important battles. The first battle was against the Umayyads, who opposed Ali as caliph. It became known as the Battle of the Camel, because Muhammad's widow, Aisha, rode a camel during the fighting. Ali beat his opponents, including Aisha. The Battle of the Camel was the first major battle between Muslims.

Ali's next conflict was against an Umayyad named Muawiyah, who was a relative of Uthman. Ali was defeated when Muawiyah's warriors entered the battle with copies of the Koran strapped to their spears, a sight that halted the pious members of Ali's group. Ali reached an agreement with the Umayyads, but his status as a leader was destroyed; Ali's former supporters killed him in AD 661, while he was standing in the doorway of a mosque in Kufa.

Muawiyah became the next caliph, when Ali's eldest son relinquished any claim to the title. Still, many other Muslims continued to support Ali and his descendants as the true caliphs. They came to be known as Shiites.

Pictured here is a modern painting of the mosque and holy shrine of Husayn, son of Ali, Muhammad's son-in-law and the fourth caliph who was murdered with his fighters in Karbala in what is now Iraq.

Yet another major battle was waged when Muawiyah died. Ali's second son Husayn was persuaded to pursue the position of caliph. He set off into the desert with seventy-two members of his family and supporters. Upon arriving at Kufa, however, they discovered that they had been tricked. Yazid, the current caliph, and 4,000 of his supporters surrounded Husayn's party and deprived them of food and water. Demanding immediate surrender, Yazid's warriors held their arrows and weapons in position to kill Husayn's family and his followers.

But Husayn's group resisted. They dug a ditch behind themselves to prevent their own escape as they prepared to fight to the death. As the massacre began, Husayn's warrior brother, 'Abbas, fought his way through the crowd to reach the Euphrates River. He wanted to bring water to the women and children in his group who were dying from thirst. On his way back, he was attacked and his hand was cut off. Ultimately, every member of the party was killed. Husayn himself was the last man standing. Legend says that he died holding a sword in one hand and the Koran in the other.

The massacre became an important event to the Shiites. It was an epic battle, with themes of betrayal, pain, martyrdom, and, finally, redemption. It has sometimes been compared to the life of Jesus Christ, which holds a similar importance for Christians. The shrine-tombs of the two brothers are among the most important shrines for Shiite Muslims, a destination of pilgrimages from across the Islamic world.

The 'Abbasids

The descendants of 'Abbas, known as the 'Abbasids, or Sunnis, revolted against the Umayyads. Beginning with Abu'l-'Abbas, the 'Abbasids ushered in the golden era of the Islamic Empire that lasted until 1258. After the secular (nonreligious) lifestyle of the Umayyads, the 'Abbasids prided themselves on following the Islamic faith. But they were also worldly and decadent.

'Abbas's successor, Abu Ja'far, also known as al-Mansur, moved the capital of Islam from Damascus to Baghdad. Soon the medieval city, which was surrounded by three walls and a double moat, housed a population of one million Muslims and was a center of scholarship. By this time, the caliph was considered no mere successor to the Prophet, but rather a deputy to Allah. The palace of the caliph had a golden dome and gate and boasted such

This photograph shows the Shiite shrine to 'Abbas, who was Muhammad's grandson and was himself a Shiite leader.

riches as a solid silver tree with golden branches and singing mechanical birds.

Often called the "Paris of the ninth century" by historians, Baghdad became the intellectual and cultural capital of the world. While Europe was in the depths of the Dark Ages, Muslim scholars in Baghdad were translating texts from Greece, Persia, and India. They studied law and theology, medicine, and pharmacology. Public schools and hospitals were built and organized; the fields of astronomy, poetry, music, art, and mathematics prospered. The feel of the 'Abbasid Empire was captured in the tales of *A Thousand and One Nights*, commonly called *Arabian Nights*, some of

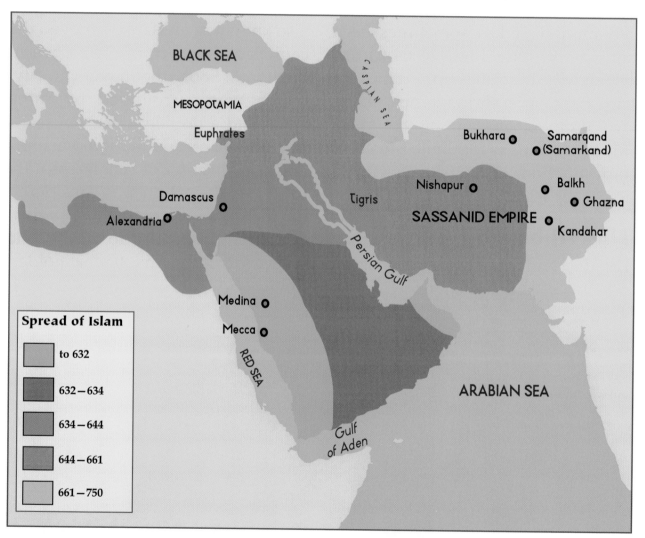

The spread of Islam after Muhammad's death was rapid, and within only a few decades it had followers on three continents: Asia, Africa, and Europe. As the Muslim civilization developed further, it absorbed and preserved much of the knowledge of the ancient world, which was then translated into Arabic. Muslims were also responsible for the development of algebra, the concept of zero, and the invention of the astrolabe and quadrant (instruments later used by European explorers), among other achievements.

The Golden Age of Islam

The Golden Age of Islam emerged after the founding of Baghdad in the mid-eighth century and spanned some 400 years. This period of enlightenment, scholarship, and intellectualism thrived only once the Islamic empire experienced tremendous territorial growth largely without the threat of outside attack. Trade throughout the empire grew, and Arabic was used as the standard language. The Islamic faith united the Muslim people. Although the accomplishments of this period in Islamic history are too numerous to mention here, some of its greatest achievements are advancements in science, mathematics, and artistic culture. Medical science became a study based in experimentation and observation, rather then one based in speculation. The concept of "zero" as well as the science of chemistry were both introduced for the first time. The world's first observatory was built; astronomical data were collected. In addition, the Muslims developed the astrolabe, an instrument for determining the position of celestial bodies.

This manuscript illumination of a ship in the Persian Gulf dates from AD 1237 and was found in Baghdad. The original manuscript is now located in France's National Library in Paris.

which was written during its height. Glittering and glamorous, many of the stories feature personalities from the time such as the scandalous poet Abu Nuwas.

Baghdad was also the center for trade in the Middle East. Ships carried goods to and from India, Ceylon (Sri Lanka), and China. Camel caravans crossed the desert sands to bring back delights from Persia, Arabia, Egypt, and Syria.

But Baghdad's calm and prosperity was about to end. Jews and Christians began to oppress Muslim groups. Because Muslim territories had become too large to govern effectively, civil wars and political disputes threatened their stability. The Buyids, a Persian Shiite family,

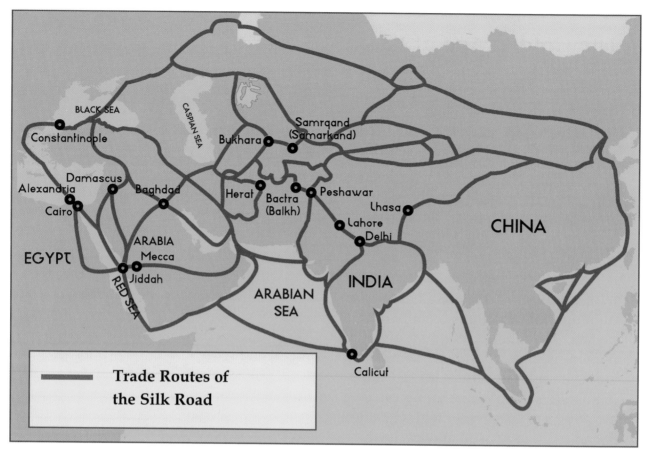

By AD 600, Muslims controlled most of the trade routes known as the Silk Road, though their control and the road's use would diminish over the following centuries. The road made a comeback around AD 1200, after the invasion of Mongol hordes throughout central Asia. Having gained control of the region, Mongol forces enforced the routes, which again became safe for speedy travel by caravan. The Mongol development of a postal relay system (*yam*), in which official communications were sent, led to maintained caravan stations along crucial points where travelers could find water and shelter.

gained enormous power. They took over and installed secular rule for a century, keeping the Sunni caliph merely as a religious figurehead. In response, the Seljuks, a Sunni family from Turkey, assumed power and attempted to restore traditional religious values in the Muslim world.

For centuries, the Islamic Empire had been battling Western Christian kingdoms. The united nations of Europe, under the leadership of the Holy Roman Empire, launched a number of religious wars against Islam. Known as the Crusades, these religious wars were fought between Christians and Muslims. During the eleventh century, the Christian Crusaders entered the eastern Mediterranean region en masse. They were eventually fought off, but the Muslim Empire was weakened.

6 CONQUERORS FROM OUTSIDE

In 1258 Hülegü, Mongol leader and a grandson of Genghis Khan, and his followers conquered Baghdad after a deadly seven-week siege. The last 'Abbasid caliph was kicked to death. According to some accounts, 800,000 corpses were stacked in the streets. Baghdad was devastated; its treasures and artifacts were destroyed or stolen.

More than a century later, the devastation continued. Another band of Mongols, this time led by Timur (also known as Timur the Lame, or Tamerlane), conquered the once illustrious city of Baghdad in 1393 and again in 1401.

The Ottoman Empire

Meanwhile, the Ottoman Turks, from their base in Turkey, were gaining power in the West, in present-day Europe. During the 1530s, Süleyman the Magnificent added the city of Baghdad to his empire. For a brief period, the Persians gained control of the region surrounding Baghdad; but otherwise, the Ottomans controlled the entire Mesopotamian region until 1918. The central provinces of Mosul, Baghdad, and Basra of the Ottoman Empire as well as the northern section of Shahrizor, east of the Tigris, and Al-Hasa in the south, west of the Persian Gulf, became known as Iraq.

The Turks were Sunni Muslims, and they perse-cuted the Shiites, who were the majority of the

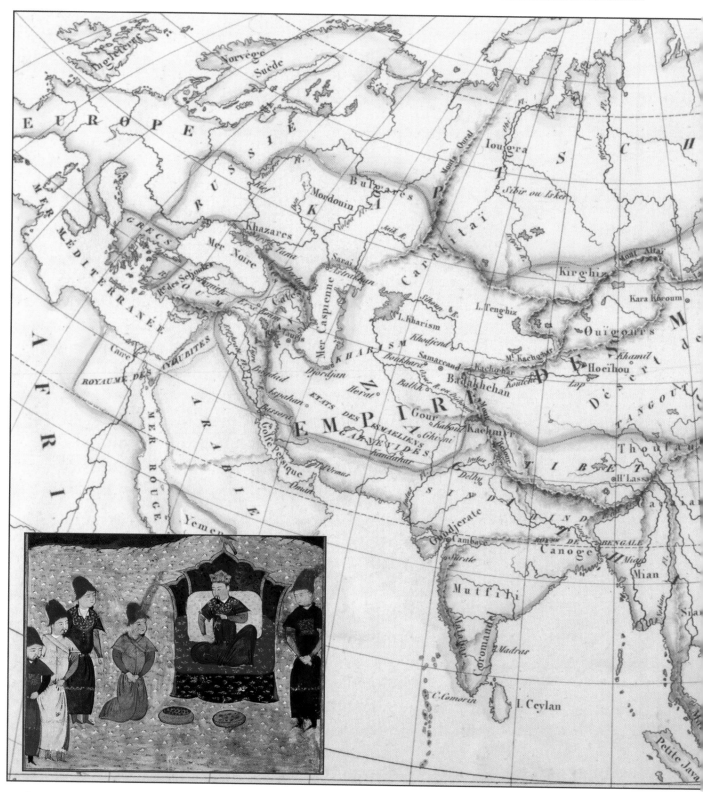

The Mongol Empire, shown at its greatest extent on this map, circa AD 1300, or about forty years after Hülegü led the siege of Baghdad, a city that had been weakened prior to invasion by flood waters that undermined its fortresses. Hülegü was a grandson of the Mongol conqueror Genghis Khan (inset), who is pictured on this fourteenth-century illustration by Rashid al-Din, now housed in the National Library of France, in Paris.

population in the region. Turkish rule increased in the provinces, making the provincial officials suspicious of government practices. Subsequently, more and more Iraqis preferred their own tribal laws and identities.

Midhat Pasha, an Ottoman governor of Iraq from 1869 to 1872, made many improvements to the region. He established reforms to help give the public a voice in government affairs. He made possible public education outside the mosques and provided for the settlement of tribes on specific lands. He also allowed the creation of newspapers, banks, and hospitals. However, the Iraqi people's commitment to tribal law and protection remained strong and intact.

Invasion from the West

By the beginning of the twentieth century, Western powers such as Germany and the United Kingdom were taking notice of the area and its abundance of natural resources. Ottoman Turks sided with Germany during World War I (1914–1918), which gave the Allies an excuse to further invade Arab territories, previously under Turkish rule. In the process of defending Persian oil fields from potential attack by the Turks, the British sent troops to the southern tip of Iraq. The British captured the

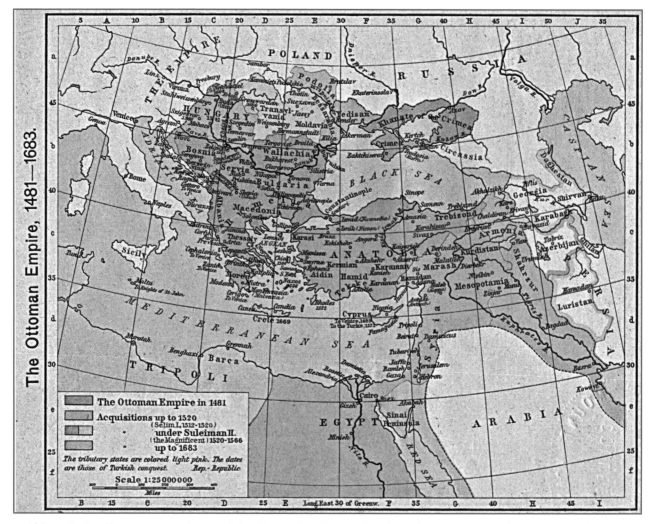

The Ottoman Empire, 1481–1683.

Although the Ottoman overthrow of the Mesopotamian region later known as Iraq (acquisitions that are shown on this historic map) helped define its borders and increase its security, by the time the Turks gained control in the 1530s the region was in turmoil. Destruction and neglect after prior invasions had disrupted or ruined irrigation systems, many people were living nomadically, and any community ties were largely tribal. Under the administration of Süleyman the Magnificent, however, trade increased, buildings were restored or rebuilt, and the economy and overall living conditions of most people improved.

province of Basra, and then, buoyed by their success, attempted to seize Baghdad in 1915.

Some historians consider the British effort to invade Baghdad as one of the most bungled military operations in British history. British troops marched north along the Tigris River and came within twenty-five miles (forty kilometers) of Baghdad. Once there, the British encountered massive resistance by the Turkish troops. The British were forced to retreat downriver to a desolate town called Al Kut (or Kut al Imara), which was a British stronghold. There, after some minor fighting with the Turks, the British were held under siege for more than four months. In the midst of the siege, Major General Charles Townshend, the British commander, overestimated his supplies, thinking they would last for months. Several efforts were made by the British military to send reinforcements and resources, but all attempts failed, resulting in the loss of nearly 23,000 British soldiers. By the time Townshend surrendered on April 29, 1916, his 8,000 troops were malnourished or sick with disease. Many of them died while marching without water to labor camps located in Turkey. Eventually, by 1917, the British were successful in capturing Baghdad.

Postwar Boundaries

After much debate at the peace conferences that followed World War I, the regions of Mesopotamia were divided among the victors. The British kept the three Ottoman provinces of Basra, Baghdad, and Mosul, thus creating modern Iraq. The British also claimed Palestine. The French took Syria and Lebanon. Some historians blame many of the problems of the Middle East on these divisions. In Iraq alone, the British placed the Shiites, Sunnis, and Kurds—three groups with a history of violent hatred for one another—together, under one nation.

The Sunnis and the Shiites so hated the British that they were able to put aside their own differences in a united revolt against their new leaders. They rallied around Sherif Husayn's son Faisal, who had set up a government in Syria. The revolt lasted three months, and was far more severe than the British could have imagined. In the end, the British lost 2,269 men and Iraq lost 8,450.

The British had planned to rule Iraq through an Arab king whom they could control. After great debate, they agreed to let Faisal rule after an election in 1921. Although the British probably staged the election, Faisal won with 96 percent of the vote. Faisal did hold some claim to the office; he was a descendant of Muhammad and had previously fought for Arab nationalism in the earlier revolt against the Turks. Faisal was also in conflict with the French, which made him useful to the British.

By 1930, the British agreed to terminate their control over Iraq—at least officially. In 1932 Iraq gained full independence and was admitted into the League of Nations. The British, however, continued their influence in Iraq by placing Royal Air Force squadrons on bases northwest of Baghdad. Around this same time, oil, discovered in the 1910s,

CYPRUS
LEBANON
Beirut 1920
PALESTINE
SYRIA
JORDAN
IRAQ
1920
IRAN
SAUDI ARABIA
Persian
Gulf

Post–World War I Borders 1918–1920

The map pictured here clearly defines new post–World War I boundaries in the Middle East as divided by the British and French as a part of the Treaty of Versailles. For many, the new divisions were culturally unpleasant as they placed side by side people of varied religions who would, in more ordinary circumstances, be living apart.

became an immediate source of revenue for its burgeoning economy. Still, the new income did not usher in a period of Iraqi peace.

On the contrary, as King Faisal admitted in a confidential memo in 1933, "There [are] no Iraqi people, but unimaginable masses of human beings devoid of any patriotic ideas, imbued with religious traditions and absurdities, connected by no common tie, giving ear to evil, prone to anarchy, and perpetually ready to rise against any government whatsoever." It was in this manner that Iraq entered into its era of independence.

7 | THE TURMOIL WITHIN

King Faisal, who ruled until his death in 1933, accurately predicted a state of revolution in Iraq, although he did not live to see it. When he died, his son, King Ghazi, took the throne. Ghazi died just five years later in a car crash, leaving his four-year-old son, Faisal II, as heir to the throne. But the boy was still too young to take the crown, so his uncle, Abd al-Ilah, stood in for him as regent and crown prince.

An Unstable Landscape

Meanwhile, ongoing tensions with the Kurds, a large group of people living in northern Iraq, continued. The Kurds had been promised an independent state—Kurdistan—by the British and the Allied powers at the peace talks after World War I. But the plan, which called for territory to be taken from Iraq, Turkey, and Iran, was never fulfilled. By 1926, Kurdish areas such as the city of Mosul were taken from Turkey and brought under Iraqi rule. To this day, the Kurdish people desire their own land, boundaries, and the right to govern themselves, and have since shed much blood in that pursuit.

Another issue was caused by the increased power of the Iraqi military, which had become more politically active. In 1936, military leaders staged a coup, overturned the Iraqi government, but left King Ghazi in place. Other coups followed, and the politicians and the military split into two major factions or groups: One was pro-British and the other was pro-German.

In 1941, during World War II (1939–1945), the leader of the pro-German faction, Rashid Ali al-Kaylani, was overconfident because of Nazi leader Adolf Hitler's successful devastation of Europe. Rashid Ali refused to provide support to the British war efforts. Britain retaliated by invading Iraq. Rashid Ali attempted to overthrow British power once and for all. The two major Iraqi leaders, Crown Prince Abd al-Ilah and Prime Minister Nuri al-Said, were forced into exile, fleeing Iraq. Rashid Ali became prime minister. The pro-German rebels were quickly defeated, despite military support from the Axis Powers (the countries allied with Germany during World War II). Abd al-Ilah and Nuri al-Said returned, and four of the rebels were hanged. Later, Iraq supported the Allied powers and declared war on Germany.

Vice-Premier and Interior Minister Colonel Abdel Salem Aref (right, with raised hand) of Iraq addresses a crowd in An Najaf, Iraq, in 1958. The packed streets below are hung with streamers hailing the Iraqi revolution. The goal of Aref's visit to An Najaf was to explain the objectives of the revolution to the area's Shiite Muslim population.

The Iraqi monarchy remained standing, but was unstable without British support. The United Kingdom was seriously weakened during World War II and could not afford to continue backing the unstable Iraqi monarchy.

Now that it was time for Iraq to support itself as a nation, it intended to maintain friendly relations with the West. In 1945 the Arab League was established, with Iraq as a founding member. Its purpose was to provide some unity among the Arab nations. That same year, Iraq joined the United Nations. In defense against the Soviet Union and its rising power, Iraq joined with Turkey, and later with Iran and Pakistan, to sign the Baghdad Pact, a mutual defense treaty. Then, in 1958, Iraq and Jordan formed the Arab Federation to counter the socialist United Arab Republic in Syria and Egypt.

Meanwhile, Iraq's oil revenue was increasing, helping to stabilize its economy. In 1951 Iraq's neighbor Iran nationalized its oil industry, losing its favorable position with international oil companies. Iraq saw an opportunity to grab the majority of the international oil business and boost its economy. Although oil sales brought considerable riches to the government, some historians believe that the industry may have ultimately destabilized Iraq, as well as the Middle East.

Oil was discovered in Iraq early in the twentieth century, making the country, like the rest of the Middle East, a valuable contributor to the world's oil-seeking Western countries such as the Untied States. This contemporary photo of northern Iraq shows a section of the country mostly occupied by Kurds.

Increased wealth meant that governments could build larger armies—military forces more connected to supporting the government than its people. Taxes, as well as public opinion, meant little to a government that could buy its own army and vast security forces. As Iraq's wealth increased, so did its authoritarian control.

In 1953 young Faisal II became king, although Iraq's actual leadership was still in the hands of Abd al-Ilah and Nuri al-Said. As a measure of his power, Prime Minister Nuri al-Said banned all political parties in 1954. Murmurs of opposition began to rumble throughout the territory. At the same time, the government appeared suspicious in the eyes of the public because of its ties to the West. When the French, British, and Israelis attacked Egypt in 1956, the

Saudi Arabian delegates El Zerekly *(center)* and Sheikh Youssef Yassin *(right)*, acting minister for foreign affairs, are pictured in this photo from 1945 as they sign the Arab League Charter in Cairo, Egypt.

Iraqi tide of anti-Western sentiment rose even further.

Revolution

The revolution came on July 14, 1958. Rebel troops led by Abd al-Karim Qasim stormed the palace in Baghdad, setting fire to it with artillery. Young King Faisal II, just twenty-three, tried to escape with his family and advisers. But as the group burst free from the burning palace, a brigade of rebel sharpshooters encircled them with submachine gunfire. The rebels were the only survivors.

For the next ten years, Iraq was in turmoil resulting in coups, counter-coups, and chaos. Qasim declared Iraq a republic, not a monarchy, and appointed himself prime minister. A new constitution was outlined, and Islam became Iraq's official religion.

Iraq was declared a part of the Arab nation, with Arabs and Kurds as partners in the homeland. And although it was a valiant effort to become a stabilized nation, Iraq continued to be hindered by repeated conspiracies, revolts, and violence. In 1963 Qasim and his regime were overthrown in a bloody counterrevolution in which 5,000 people, including Qasim, were tortured and killed.

During this time, the Kurdish uprising was gaining momentum. One Iraqi leader after another was killed or exiled. The West was, by now, considered completely pro-Israel and hated by most of the Arab world. Meanwhile, in the United States, Allan Dulles, the director of the Central Intelligence Agency (CIA), named Iraq the most dangerous place on earth.

8 SADDAM HUSSEIN

On July 16, 1979, Saddam Hussein at-Tikriti became president and chairman of the Revolutionary Command Council. In many ways, he was the perfect candidate for the role he was about to create: despotic dictator, or a ruler who has absolute authority.

Hussein was born in the village of Ouija in northern Iraq on April 28, 1937. Hussein's father was a peasant farmer who died when Hussein was a baby. Young Hussein's mother raised him; she had the support of the rest of the family. They were Sunni Muslims. Although Hussein's relatives were not wealthy, many held powerful military positions.

As a young man, Hussein joined the Ba'th Party, an ambitious Arab nationalist group with a socialist ideology. In 1968, after ten years of political chaos in Iraq, including the 1963 overthrow of Abd al-Karim Qasim, the Ba'th Party definitively overthrew the regime and seized power. Unlike previous regimes, the Ba'th Party took no chances with any opposition. Former leaders, if they were lucky, were escorted to the airport with guns held to their backs. Others were killed outright.

Ten years after the revolution, on July 16, 1979, Hussein officially became president of Iraq. Even before Hussein's inauguration, his opponents were at risk. In one of his first official meetings with party leaders,

Saddam Hussein, pictured here in 1981, has often been criticized by Westerners for his mistreatment of Iraqis, often violating their human rights. However, many Iraqis offer unquestionable support for their leader.

Hussein began his purge. After a planned dialogue, in which one of his men called out that Hussein had been too merciful, Hussein began calling names of suspected traitors, who were then removed from the room. While weeping, Hussein invited the remaining group, now terrified, to join the firing squad that executed their colleagues. Hussein was setting a precedent that left little room for dissent (disagreement) or opposition. His opponents had been either eliminated or terrorized into silence.

The Iran-Iraq War

In 1980 Iraq went to war with Iran, a nation that had previously undergone an Islamic revolution. One year before, the Ayatollah Ruhollah Khomeini became Iran's religious and political leader. Khomeini had returned from a fourteen-year exile from Iran and seized power from Mohammad Reza Shah Pahlavi, the shah (king) of Iran. Khomeini, a militant Shiite, wanted the Shiite community in Iraq to join in his Islamic

A member of Iraq's Ba'th Party, Abdul Baqi al-Sa'doun salutes Iraqis parading in military fatigues in Baghdad on the thirty-ninth anniversary of Iraq's February 8, 1963, revolution. Iraqis pledged readiness to fight with the Palestinians and defend the country against any attack by United States president George W. Bush.

Iraqi soldiers are pictured on the front line in this photograph, circa 1980, during the Iran-Iraq War in Basra, Iraq. Though Iran had gained an early lead in the war, the conflict ended after Saddam Hussein authorized the military use of poison gas in 1988.

revolution. When war began, Iraq, which had one-third of the population of Iran, was quickly at such a disadvantage that the United States and other Western nations feared an Iranian victory. They came to Iraq's aid, supplying intelligence, weaponry, U.S. naval ships, and even satellite photos of Iranian military positions. Unknown at the time, the United States was also selling weapons to Iran in the hopes of gaining the release of seventy American citizens who were taken hostage there in a terrorist act in 1979. (This became public knowledge during the Iran-Contra affair, a scandal that rocked the United States in 1987.) After Iraq began using poison gas on the Iranians in 1988, Iran called for a truce.

The war devastated Iraq, with hundreds of thousands dead and some $77 billion owed to various countries. But Iraq's military power had never been greater, and neither had Hussein's opinion of his own power.

Late in 1989, Hussein decided that the United States no longer served his needs. He expelled U.S. CIA officials and moved to sever completely all contact with the United States.

Desert Storm

In August of 1990, Hussein directed Iraqi forces to invade Kuwait, angry that the nation was lowering the global price of oil by overproducing it and flooding the international market. Hussein also allegedly wanted to take over two tiny Kuwaiti islands that blocked Iraq's access to the Persian Gulf. Whatever Hussein's reasoning, Iraq's official plan was for a minimal invasion to settle a border dispute. However, at the last minute, Hussein changed his mind and ordered a full-scale invasion of Kuwait.

Soon it was evident that this choice was a mistake. Within days, the member countries of the United Nations unanimously opposed the hostile actions taken by Iraq to increase its size and power by seizing another country. In response, the United Nations imposed sanctions (controls) against Iraq, limiting Iraqi trade. Imported goods were halted

This current Central Intelligence Agency (CIA) map shows the small country of Kuwait and its land boundaries with Iraq and Saudi Arabia. Now almost fully recovered from its 1990–1991 conflict with Iraq, Kuwait is in the process of reviving its economy.

from entering the nation, and oil exports were no longer bought from the country.

In December, under the direction of U.S. president George H. W. Bush, the United Nations sent a joint military force into Saudi Arabia under the name Operation Desert Shield. Iraq was ordered to withdraw from Kuwait by January 15, 1991, but Hussein did not retreat. On January 17, 1991, Operation Desert

This CIA map shows Iraq and its current land boundaries with Saudi Arabia, Syria, Turkey, Iran, and Kuwait. According to recent statistics, Iraq has the second-largest oil reserves in the world, natural resources that have allowed the country to fortify its military forces and arms, as well as fund an invasion of Kuwait in 1990. At the time of this writing, international speculation has increased as to whether or not Iraq has begun to develop weapons of mass destruction, by biological, chemical, or nuclear means.

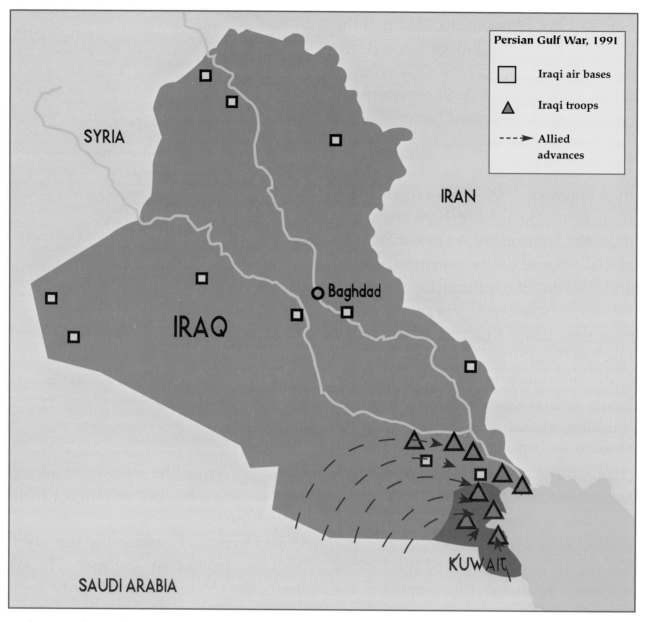

This map shows allied advances on Iraq during the Persian Gulf War, a conflict that was originally caused by Iraq's invasion of Kuwait in 1990, an attempt made by Saddam Hussein to gain its oil reserves. A coalition of more than 700,000 ground troops from the United States, Britain, France, Egypt, Saudi Arabia, and Syria helped force Iraqi soldiers out of Kuwait by 1991.

Shield became Operation Desert Storm (the Persian Gulf War) with a launch of air missile attacks on Baghdad. On February 24, ground forces landed in an effort to retake Kuwait. Although a cease-fire was called on February 28, 1991, Hussein did not officially accept the agreement until April.

The consequences of the attack were devastating to the Iraqi people. Baghdad, a wealthy and modern city, was plunged back into the dark ages. Its generators were destroyed. Without electricity, sewage treatment became impossible. Soon the Tigris River was fetid and filthy. Many buildings were bombed and destroyed. Eventually basic necessities were restored, but Baghdad has yet to return to its prior level of operability.

Rebellion

Faced with a failing economy and a devastated nation, Iraq was forced to surrender. The Gulf War was over, but the chaos was not. Angry soldiers retreating from Kuwait lost respect for Hussein. They felt unprotected and betrayed by their leader. Inspired in part by U.S. president Bush's speeches intentionally urging rebellion, a revolt arose to overthrow Hussein and the Ba'th Party. The violence spread quickly across southern Iraq. Hussein's portrait was shot at in outrageous acts of insubordination. Security forces were shot down and killed or stabbed to death.

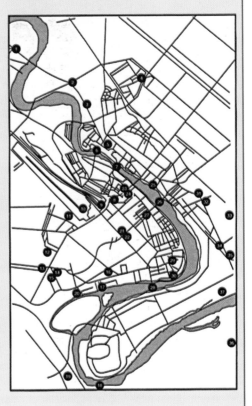

Downtown Baghdad

(First Twenty-four hours of the war)

1. Directorate of Military Intelligence
2, 5, 8, 13, 34. Telephone switching station.
3. Ministry of Defense National Computer Complex
4. Electrical transfer station
6. Ministry of Defense HQ
7. Ashudad highway bridge
9. Railroad yard
10. Muthena airfield (military section)
11. New Iraq Air Force HQ
12. Iraqi Intelligence Service HQ
14. Secret Police complex
15. Army storage depot
16. Republican Guard HQ
17. New Presidential Palace
18. Electrical power station
19. SRBM assembly factors (Scud)
20. Baath party HQ
21. Government Conference center
22. Ministry of Industry and Military Production
23. Ministry of Propaganda
24. TV Transmitter
25, 31. Communication relay station
26. Jumhuriya highway bridge
27. Government Control Center South
28. Karada highway bridge (14th July bridge)
29. Presidential Palace Command Center
30. Presidential Palace Command Bunker
32. Secret Police HQ
33. Iraqi Intelligence Service Regional HQ
35. National Air Defense Operations Center
36. Ad Dawrah oil refinery
37. Electrical power plant

During the first twenty-four hours of the war, coalition aircraft struck critical targets in Saddam's capital and elsewhere. Weeks of fighting remained, but the initial attack was so overwhelming that Iraq was unable to mount a coherent military response thereafter. First day targets in Baghdad are numbered on the map.

Downtown Baghdad, seen here in this 1991 map featured in *Decisive Force*, a book by Richard G. Davis, a member of the U.S. Air Force, shows initial targets in the city on January 17–18, 1991. The combination of attacks from the air never allowed the city to recover long enough to retaliate.

Meanwhile, in the northern region of Iraq, the Kurds began a carefully planned revolution. One group of Kurdish rebels gained access to a stone fortress known as Central Security Headquarters. Inside they found instruments of torture, many

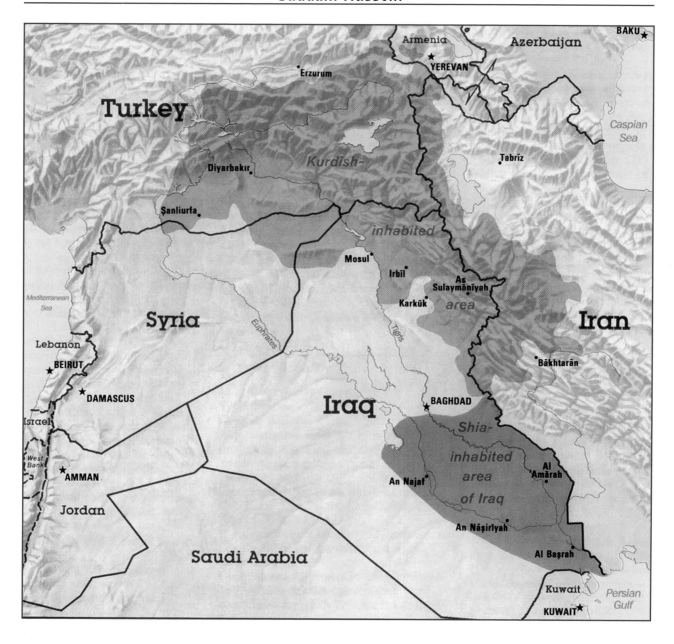

This 1992 CIA map *(above)* shows dissident areas of Iraq at that time, with shaded areas depicting sections of the country inhabited by Kurds and Shiite Muslims. The top photograph to the left shows an Iraqi prisoner of war with an American soldier in southern Iraq in 1991. The lower photograph shows damage to a bridge in Baghdad during the Persian Gulf War.

of them still smeared with blood. The 400 Ba'th Party members found in the building were each massacred by the enraged Kurds.

Although the United States had encouraged the rebellion, it backed away from helping the Kurdish rebels. Furious, Hussein began attacking Kurds and Shiites alike, killing thousands. To prevent further disaster, the United States called for a no-fly zone to protect the Kurds who were fleeing Hussein by the thousands.

UNSCOM and Sanctions

At the end of the Gulf War, U.S. intelligence officers learned that Hussein may have been developing chemical and biological weapons. In fact, Hussein had already used poison and nerve gas against the Kurds, with devastating effects. Therefore, full economic sanctions against Iraq had been declared as part of the cease-fire agreement. The sanctions would be lifted only when a full-scale accounting of Iraq's biological and chemical weapons was conducted. Called the United Nations Special Commission on Iraq, or UNSCOM, the operation was expected to be a quick solution to the growing fear of Hussein's ability to manufacture weapons of mass destruction. However, the sanctions remained in place as Hussein continually

Iraqis demonstrate in Baghdad in November 1998, calling for the expulsion of United Nations arms inspectors and accusing them of being spies. Demonstrators chanted "UNSCOM spies and Zionists out!" The protest came as Iraq and the United Nations were locked in a standoff over arms inspections after Baghdad decided to halt cooperation with UNSCOM.

outmaneuvered the UNSCOM officers in their inspection efforts of
Iraqi military facilities.

In 1994, Iraqi forces invaded
Kuwait again, but Hussein withdrew
when the United States threatened to
retaliate. One year later, Hussein was
empowered with an unlikely 99.96
percent of the vote. In the fall of 1996,
one Kurdish group asked Hussein
for assistance to defeat its Kurdish
enemies. At this, Hussein's power
was reestablished in northern Iraq.
From his new point of operations, he
fired at patrolling U.S. and allied
planes in a no-fly zone. And in retal-
iation, the United States destroyed
military targets in southern Iraq.

UN sanctions against Iraq were
having a devastating effect on the
civilian population. The United
Nation's Food and Agricultural
Commission estimated that more
than 500,000 children had died as a
result. In December of 1996, some of
the sanctions were lifted in an oil-for-
food exchange.

Although many individuals had
tried to oust Hussein, none had succeeded. Many of them have paid
dearly for their efforts, often dying
under torture. Hungry, demoralized,
and terrorized, the citizens of Iraq
remained under the threat of a leader
who cared little for the death and
misery of his people.

Many government officials
throughout the world believed
Hussein was hiding mass graves in
Iraq. His troops have killed and
imprisoned Kurds in concentration
camps. Many also believed that he had
ties to the Al Qaeda terrorist network
and Osama bin Laden, alleged master-
mind of terrorist acts throughout the
world, including the attacks on the
United States on September 11, 2001.

In 2003, after months of weapons
inspections and talks with UN officials, no determination was made
regarding the status of Iraq's
weapons programs. Because of this
ambiguity and Iraq's alleged ties to
the terrorist strikes of September 11,
President George W. Bush and
British prime minister Tony Blair
launched a war on Iraq to oust
Hussein from power. Together, U.S.
and British forces swiftly captured
Baghdad. President Bush declared
victory over Iraq on May 1 of that
same year, and U.S. troops captured
Hussein in December. Today, U.S. ,
British, and other allied forces
remain in the country with the hope
of establishing peace there, despite
its long history of bloodshed and
conflict.

TIMELINE

5000 BC Mesopotamia flourishes

3300 BC Writing begins in Sumer

2500 BC Egyptians build the Pyramids

2400 BC Assyrian Empire is established

2334 BC Rule of Sargon I

1750 BC Rule of Hammurabi in Babylonia

638 BC Approximate birth of Persian prophet Zoroaster (Zarathrustra)

600 BC Cyrus the Great establishes the Achaemenid Empire

563 BC Approximate birth of Buddha

331 BC Alexander the Great captures Babylon

323 BC Alexander the Great dies

AD 200 Sassanians rise to power

AD 226 Approximate date Zoroastrianism is established

AD 313 Christianity is accepted by the Romans

AD 570 Birth of Muhammad

AD 600 Roman, Parthian, and Kushan Empires flourish

AD 610 Muhammad's first revelation

AD 622 Buddhism begins its spread from India to Asia

AD 625 Muslims control Mesopotamia and Persia

AD 632 Death of Muhammad

AD 633–700 Followers of Islam start to spread their faith

AD 685 Shiite revolt in Iraq

AD 750 Abbasid caliphate, Iraq

AD 751 Arabs learn papermaking from the Chinese

AD 762 City of Baghdad is founded

AD 1215 Genghis Khan captures China and moves westward

AD 1220 Mongols sack Bukhara, Samarkand, and Tashkent

AD 1258 Mongols sack Baghdad

AD 1379 Timur invades Iraq

AD 1387 Timur conquers Persia

AD 1453 Ottoman Empire captures Constantinople and begins overtaking Asia

AD 1498 Vasco da Gama reaches India

AD 1526 Babur establishes Mughal Empire

AD 1534 Ottomans seize Iraq

AD 1554 First Russian invasion into central Asia

AD 1632 Taj Mahal is built

AD 1739 Nadir Shah invades the Mughal Empire, sacks Delhi

AD 1740 Ahmad Shah Durrani founds kingdom in Afghanistan

AD 1858 British rule is established in India

AD 1932 Saudi Arabia is founded by 'Abd al-'Aziz Al Sa'ud

AD 1947 India declares its independence; East/West Pakistan succession

AD 1979 Saddam Hussein becomes president of Iraq

AD 1980–1988 Iran-Iraq War

AD 1990 Iraq invades Kuwait

AD 2002 UN Security Council requires Iraq to discard weapons of mass destruction

AD 2003 President George W. Bush declares war on Iraq in March and U.S. forces continue to oocupy the country

GLOSSARY

Allied (powers) Countries united against Germany in World War I and against the Axis powers in World War II.

authoritarian Relating to or favoring a concentration of power in a government leader.

caliph A successor of Muhammad as secular and spiritual head of Islam.

coup (coup d'état) A French term meaning "blow to the state" that refers to a sudden, unexpected overthrow of a government by outsiders.

cuneiform The alphabetic language first developed by the ancient Sumerians that is composed of wedge-shaped characters.

dictatorship A form of government in which one person or a small group holds absolute power.

exile To banish or expel from one's country or home, usually for political reasons.

fundamentalism A movement or attitude stressing strict and literal adherence to a set of basic principles, usually associated with religious beliefs.

Islam The religious faith of Muslims, including belief in Allah as the sole deity and in Muhammad as his prophet.

khan A title denoting leadership or royalty, especially in central Asia; similar to king, caesar, or tsar.

lapis lazuli A semiprecious stone, usually a rich blue in color, traded during ancient times.

martyrdom The act of suffering death rather than sacrificing one's own religious principals.

mosque A building used for prayer by Muslims.

Muslim A person who practices the religion of Islam.

nomad A person who roams from place to place, usually seasonally, in order to sustain himself or herself.

Old Testament The first part of the Christian Bible, containing the books of the Jewish canon of scripture.

Persian One of the major language groups spoken in central Asia, which includes Pashto and Tajik.

pious Reverently religious; devout.

propaganda The spread of ideas, information, or rumors for the purposes of helping or injuring an institution, a cause, or a person. Governments sometimes use propaganda to sway public opinion.

Semitic Of, or relating to, the ancient language group that includes both Hebrew and Arabic.

Shiite The Muslim sect whose members believe that leadership of the Islamic community should be through dynastic succession from the prophet Muhammad.

Silk Road A series of travel routes through central Asia linking China and India to western Europe.

Socialism A government system that advocates collective ownership of land and and distribution of goods.

Sunni The Muslim sect whose members believe that Muhammad's successor should be elected.

terrorism The use or threat of violence to create fear or alarm.

ziggurat An ancient Mesopotamian temple tower and shrine, usually in the shape of a step pyramid.

Zionism A movement that supports the establishment of a Jewish community in Palestine.

FOR MORE INFORMATION

American-Arab Anti-Discrimination
    Committee
4201 Connecticut Avenue
Washington, DC 20008
(202) 244-2990
e-mail: adc@adc.org
Web site: http://www.adc.org/

Center for Middle Eastern Studies
The University of Texas at Austin
1 University Station, #F9400
Austin, TX 78712-1193
(512) 471-3881
e-mail: cmes@menic.utexas.edu
Web site: http://menic.utexas.edu/
    menic/

Iraq Action Coalition (IAC)
7309 Haymarket Lane
Raleigh, NC 27615
e-mail: IAC@leb.net
Web site: http://iraqaction.org/

Web Sites

Due to the changing nature of Internet
links, the Rosen Publishing Group, Inc.,
has developed an online list of Web sites
related to the subject of this book. This
site is updated regularly. Please use this
link to access the list:

http://www.rosenlinks.com/liha/iraq/

FOR FURTHER READING

Corzine, Phylis. *Iraq* (Modern Nations
    of the World). San Diego, CA:
    Gale/Lucent Books, 2001.
Deedrick, Tami. *Mesopotamia* (Ancient
    Civilizations). Austin, TX: Raintree
    Steck-Vaughn, 2002.
Docherty. J. P. *Iraq* (Major World
    Nations). Broomall, PA: Chelsea
    House Publishers, 2002.

Kotapish, Dawn. *Daily Life in Ancient and
    Modern Baghdad*. Minneapolis, MN:
    Lerner Publications, 2000.
Nardo, Don. *The War Against Iraq*
    (American War Library). San Diego,
    CA: Gale/Lucent Books, 2001.
Shields, Charles J. *Saddam Hussein*
    (Major World Leaders). Broomall,
    PA: Chelsea House Publishers, 2002.

BIBLIOGRAPHY

Cockburn, Andrew, and Patrick
    Cockburn. *Out of the Ashes: The
    Resurrection of Saddam Hussein*. New
    York: HarperCollins, 1999.
Haj, Samira. *The Making of Iraq, 1900–
    1963*. New York: State University of
    New York Press, 1997.
Herodotus. *The Histories*. New York:
    Penguin Classics, 1999.
Hoge, James F., Jr. *How Did This Happen?
    Terrorism and the New War*. New
    York: Public Affairs, 2001.

Mansfield, Peter. *The Arabs*. Middlesex,
    England: Penguin Books, 1964.
Moscati, Sabatino. *The Face of the Ancient
    Orient: Near Eastern Civilization in
    Pre-Classical Times*. New York: Dover
    Publications, 2001.
Roux, Georges. *Ancient Iraq*. Middlesex,
    England: Penguin Books, 1964.
Wooley, C. Leonard. *The Sumerians*.
    London: Oxford University
    Press, 1965.

INDEX

About the Author

Larissa Phillips is a freelance writer in New York City. Her essays have appeared in the *New York Times* and numerous national magazines. This is her first book for young adults.

Acknowledgment

Special thanks to Aisha Khan for her generous insight into Middle Eastern and Asian history and culture.

Photo Credits

Cover (map), pp. 1 (foreground), 4–5 © 2002 Geoatlas; cover (background), pp. 1 (background), 6, 42, 52, 53, 55, 57 courtesy of General Libraries, University of Texas at Austin; cover (top left) © The Art Archive/Palace of Chihil Soutoun Isfahan/Dagli Orti; cover (bottom left), pp. 16, 20, 24 © AKG London/Erich Lessing; cover (bottom right) © AP/Wide World Photos; pp. 4 (inset), 51, 56 (bottom) © Francoise de Mulder/Corbis; pp. 8–9, 10, 12–13, 18–19, 22–23, 28–29, 36, 38, 44, 54 maps designed by Tahara Hasan; pp. 9 (inset), 15, 34, 37, 40 (inset) © AKG London; p. 11 © Pierpont Morgan Library/Art Resource, NY; p. 14 © Gianni Dagli Orti/Corbis; pp. 17, 26 © Réunion des Musées Nationaux/Art Resource, NY; p. 21 © Charles and Josette Lenars/Corbis; p. 27 © Christie's Images/Corbis; p. 30 © Ann and Bury Peerless; pp. 32–33 © Royalty Free/Corbis; p. 35 © Caroline Penn/Impact Photos; pp. 40–41 © Mary Evans Picture Library; pp. 46, 50 (top) © Bettmann/Corbis; p. 47 © Rupert Conant/Impact Photos; p. 48 © Hulton-Deutsch Collection/Corbis; p. 50 (bottom) © Reuters NewMedia Inc./Corbis; p. 56 (top) © Mohamed Ansar/Impact Photos; p. 58 © AFP/Corbis.

Series Design and Layout

Tahara Hasan

Editor

Joann Jovinelly

Photo Researcher

Elizabeth Loving